OLD ENGLISH TILE DESIGNS

FOR ARTISTS AND CRAFTSPEOPLE

Edited by
Carol Belanger Grafton

Dover Publications, Inc., New York

PUBLISHER'S NOTE

During the Middle Ages, the floors of cathedrals, churches, chapels, abbeys and monasteries were often paved with ceramic tiles decorated with a variety of figurative and geometric motifs. Scuffed and worn by roughshod worshippers through the centuries, hidden from view by floors laid over them, stolen piecemeal by unscrupulous antiquarians, or even broken up and sold as road metal, true medieval paving tiles are rarely seen in their full glory.

In the 1930's, Loyd Haberly undertook a study of floor tiles in ecclesiastical buildings in the region of Oxford, England. He attempted to reconstruct the history and technique of tilemaking, which "of all mediaeval crafts . . . was the humblest, its masterpieces being meant for the common tread." His painstaking drawings, most done *in situ* and reproduced by engravings in *Mediaeval English Pavingtiles* (published in a strictly limited edition), are the source of the present compilation.

From Haberly's now-inaccessible pictorial survey, artist Carol Belanger Grafton has chosen over 160 of the finest and most versatile motifs for the use of modern artists and craftspeople. All of the designs she has selected are worked in squares, most often as quadrants of circles within the four-sided format. Typically, each page of this book includes a full showing of a tile pattern and a detail of it, usually a quarter of the whole. This arrangement makes for instructive case studies in repeated pattern design, as well as allowing for flexibility of application.

This collection of authentic motifs from the eleventh through the fourteenth centuries is especially rich in geometric ornament that preserves traces of influences from the Continent and the Mediterranean basin. There are examples of the lattice-work beloved of the ancient Celts of the British Isles; mosaic-like patterns reminiscent of Greek and Roman pavements; and compositions that resemble the rose windows of Gothic and Romanesque structures.

Floral and foliate designs abound. The fleur-de-lis, based on the lily and probably imported to Britain by the Normans, appears frequently, as does the conventionalized oak leaf and acorn motif.

Animal forms, both real and fabulous, include lions, dogs, hares, squirrels, stags, doves, eagles, griffins and dragons, often rendered according to the canons of heraldry. Other figurative designs that will be especially useful to those who need medieval imagery are several crowned kings, a jester and a knight on horseback.

Medieval tilemakers of England used a number of techniques to decorate their wares. The usual method involved using wooden blocks cut in high relief to stamp the designs onto the surface of slabs of clay air-dried to leather hardness. It appears that the recesses imprinted in the tiles (probably by means of a type of mechanical press, at least for the large tiles) were filled in with liquid clay of a contrasting color, and then the excess slip was scraped away, resulting in an inlaid pattern. Various glazes were applied to finish the tiles, which were fired in special kilns, but the precise sequence of steps is lost. It was long believed that the tilemaker's craft was a monastic one, but Haberly disputed this. In England, the craft seems to have died out around the time of Henry VIII, who, after his break with the Roman Church, disbanded the monasteries that consumed most of the production.

Today's craftspeople in many disciplines will find countless uses for the tile designs of the Middle Ages. Ceramists, especially those creating tiles, plaques and other flat objects, will delight in the charming and authentic patterns presented here. The same designs that worked so well in medieval paving tiles can be readily adapted to linoleum, carpeting and other floor coverings, or can be cut as stencils for interior decoration on all kinds of surfaces. Designers of fabrics and wallpapers will find the tile motifs suitable for translation into their media, especially by serigraphy, photosilkscreen and batik techniques. Reduced in size (the motifs are shown here in roughly their original dimensions), the tile designs are ideal for leather tooling, woodburning, marquetry, enameling (especially cloisonné) and even stained glass. Reproduction of the solid, sharp-edged images is readily accomplished, and all of the art is copyright-free.

Copyright © 1985 by Dover Publications, Inc.
All rights reserved under Pan American and International Copyright Conventions.

Published in Canada by General Publishing Company, Ltd., 30 Lesmill Road, Don Mills, Toronto, Ontario.
Published in the United Kingdom by Constable and Company, Ltd., 10 Orange Street, London WC2H 7EG.

Old English Tile Designs for Artists and Craftspeople is a new work, first published by Dover Publications, Inc., in 1985. For this publication, Carol Belanger Grafton selected designs from *Mediaeval English Pavingtiles* by Loyd Haberly (Oxford, Basil Blackwell, 1937) and arranged them in a new sequence. The Publisher's Note was prepared specially for this edition.

DOVER *Pictorial Archive* SERIES

Manufactured in the United States of America
Dover Publications, Inc., 31 East 2nd Street, Mineola, N.Y. 11501

Library of Congress Cataloging in Publication Data

Main entry under title:

Old English tile designs for artists and craftspeople.

(Dover pictorial archive series)
"Designs [selected] from Mediaeval English pavingtiles by Loyd Haberly (Oxford, Basil Blackwell, 1937)"—T.p. verso.
1. Tiles, Medieval—England—Themes, motives. 2. Tiles—England—Themes, motives. I. Grafton, Carol Belanger. II. Haberly, Loyd, 1896– . Mediaeval English pavingtiles. III. Series.
NK4670.7.G7043   1985   738.6′0942   84-18744
ISBN 0-486-24777-5

1

2

3

4

10

11

12

13

15

16

18

24

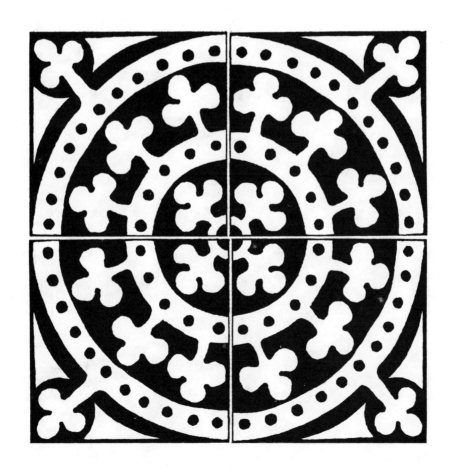

33

39

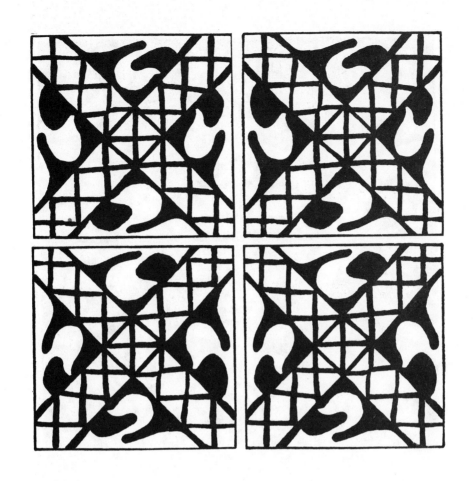

44

46

54

58

64

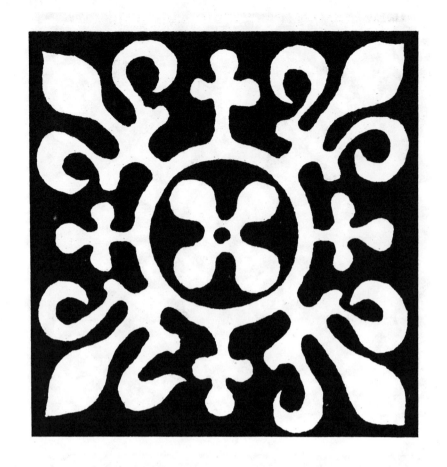

74

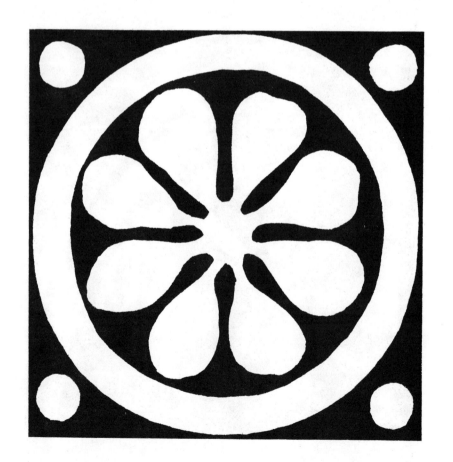

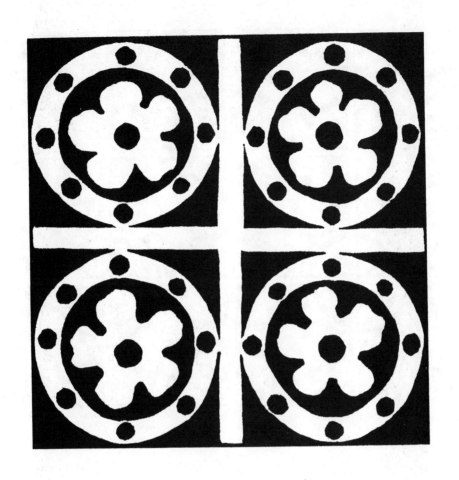

89

92

107

108

112

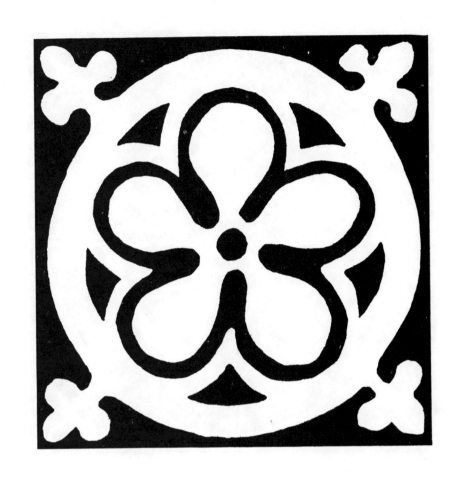

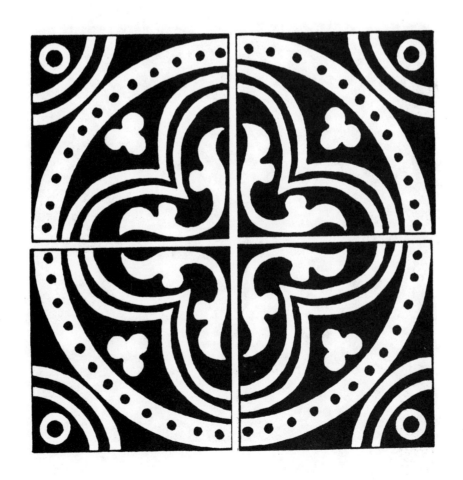

116

118

119

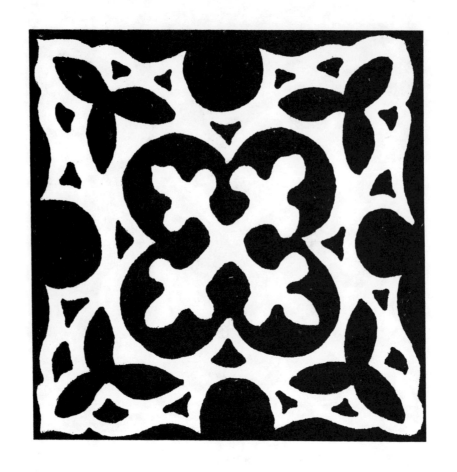